www.finishinglinepress.com

Failure to Merge

poems by

Micah Ruelle

Finishing Line Press
Georgetown, Kentucky

Failure to Merge

For Will

ACKNOWLEDGMENTS

Many thanks for my friends and colleagues at Texas State University who
helped shape the early drafts of this project. Special thanks to my ride-or-
dies who supported me during this very beautiful, but turbulent time while
crafting these poems—including but not limited to—Peter Larson, Natalie
Crary, Andrea Krause, Lauren Schiely, Laura Kraay, Allayne Thornton, Abby
Shoeman, Marilyse Figueroa, Kate Kelly, Leticia Urieta, Molly Moltzen,
Nathan Doyle, Chris Eversole, William Johnson, Jennifer Whalen, Rachel
Gray, Erin Salada, Emily Beyda, Heather McLeod, Ashton Kamburoff, and
Keith Rollins. I am deeply indebted to Aubrey Callahan Photography for
my author photos and many years of joyous friendship. And it is with deep
gratitude that I thank Jessica "Shaka" Villegas for not only designing the cover
of this collection, but for your 24 years of friendship that has deeply shaped
me as a person. It is with my whole heart that I thank my many great mentors
and friends which includes—but is not limited to—Cecily Parks, Jenny
Molberg, Octavio Quintanilla, Traci Brimhall, Wayne Miller, Kevin Prufer,
Phong Nguyen, Matthew Eck, Cyrus Cassells, Debra Monroe, and the entire
Kansas City Lady Poet Brunch Group. This project could not have come to
life if not for the inspiration and guidance of Tomás Q. Morín. And finally, big
love and thanks to my family who gave me the courage to travel this highway
and make it a home.

Publisher: Leah Maines
Editor: Christen Kincaid
Cover Art: Jessica L C Villegas
Author Photo: Aubrey Callahan, Aubrey Erin Photography
Cover Design: Christen Kincaid

Printed in the USA on acid-free paper.
Order online: www.finishinglinepress.com
also available on amazon.com

Author inquiries and mail orders:
Finishing Line Press
P. O. Box 1626
Georgetown, Kentucky 40324
U. S. A.

Table of Contents

"Interstate 35 begins at the International Border with Mexico at Laredo and terminates at Duluth, Minnesota, 148 miles southwest of the Canadian line, thus nearly affording it border-to-border status."
    —Interstate Guide

"The highway has always been your lover
and someday you may know his name"
    —Lucinda William's "Maria"

Letter 1

Dear I-35,

On Easter Sunday, my fiancé & I
drove three hours south to Laredo.
We meandered between closed,
metal garage doors of shops. Nothing
open but a few stores selling perfume,
others selling blouses & purses on racks
as high as the overhang. But downtown,
we found it: the looming white
Catholic church where his ancestors
wed for several generations.
He took me inside to meet the Mother,
& then led me to the fence
nearby where I could see the cement ravine
(I could see no water)—then past the fences
& barbed wire, to the part of you
that goes by another name. But,
I see through your disguise—
I recognize you.

Yours,
M

Letter 2

Dear M,

Always a flare
for dramatics.
I forgot that.

& for fuck's sake
don't be so formal—
call me "I."

Jokes aside,
I miss you.
Seeing you in Laredo
(from both sides)
was a nice surprise.
Love the blonde hair.
How's the beau?

Remind me
to tell you about Al—
can't now. Shit to do.

Yours,
I

WELCOME TO TEXAS

DRIVE FRIENDLY   THE TEXAS WAY

Letter 3

Dear I,

My roommate & I bought
cilantro & mint plants,
a Venus flytrap, along
with a few succulents.
For the few moments I potted
& watered them, I felt rage
subdue. The plants can't resist
my care.

There's a long list of folks
I couldn't nurture properly:
the two baby brothers,
my parents,
and a dog named Blue.
& even now, as an adult,
my care can't even find a home
in the ground. It's all sectioned off,
measured, sharing dirt
with roots & insects,
in clay pots.

Tell me about Al.

Yours,
M

P.S. The beau is well—& continues to be
the gorgeous, golden boy you'd love to hate.

P.S.S. Your potholes need as much attention as
your pen name.

Letter 4

M,

That's right—Al.

One night—very late,
I noticed headlights
pushing 80 up the exit ramp,
racing up the wrong
side. At first, I thought
it was another drunk kid.
Poor shit.
Then I recognized
the headlights: Al's.
Al is 6 foot 3 inches
of seasoned John Wayne
swagger, with enough
shots of "y'all's" & "fixin-to's"
to fill a barrel
to dunk
the modern world in.

Anyway. He's pushing 75,
& forgot which ramp was which.
The cops finally caught him.
Got things sorted. He's living
some place nice, now, I think.

You wanna talk rage?
There's something to rage about—
not your care.
Fuck your rage
& its little dog, too.

Now that we have that out of the way,
I'm sorry.
Not about your experience,
but because of your inability to see past it.
I feel sorry for you.
I hope someday you will…
This is to say, you're not trying hard enough
to love.

Yours,
I

HIT A WORKER
$10,000 FINE
LOSE YOUR LICENSE

Letter 5

I,

Remember:
we stopped talking
because of moments
like this.

I'm straddling a
"screw you"
(& your little dog, too)
& "touché"—
until I decide what's
what, here's a mix tape.

Affectionately,
M

ONE DAY YOU'RE GOING TO LOVE I-35.
UNTIL THEN,
BE CAREFUL.
BE SAFE, DRIVE SMART.

Letter 6

Dear I,

Have you heard about Ferguson?

You said I could not
see beyond my experience—
the stark white rage
white
off-handed sadness
white
eggshell white guilt
white white white
washed girl
whose mouth is a camera—
oh wait—
it's a microphone—
oh wait—
"Move!"
the whole world says,
"You're blocking — move over."

This is the "beyond"
you spoke of—
an answer?

I can see from here,
I'm behind the crowd
that can see glory
ahead—none of it white.
None of it identifiable.
The glory is moving—
it is leading.
The crowd follows.
An Exodus. I trust the ones
Who know the way.

M

Letter 7

M,

Glory? Are we in Sparta?
What do you think this is?

How about we take it down
a few notches. Fuck glory—
hell, let's settle
for safe.
Fair.
Just.
True equality.
Yeah, let's start there.

Just—whatever you're doing—
Stop. Wait to be asked.
Then proceed. In the meantime,
do your homework.

I can't do this—not when
you're like this. Glory my ass.

I

Letter 8

I,

To your first point:

you are right to correct & guide.
But why has "glory" become a dirty word?
When I know the answer,
I'll know to give it up.
But, you are right to correct
& guide. You've earned it in years.
However, you are too rough
too often, friend.

Small reliefs are just as human
as suffering.

To your second:
I'll do the work.
I'll learn to listen more closely
& put my hands to the good work.

Yours,
M

AD ASTRA PER ASPERA
[TO THE STARS THROUGH DIFFICULTY]
KANSAS WELCOMES YOU!

Letter 9

Dear M,

Now that the frustration—
old-world, pre-cement,
has cooled. Take some notes.
Consider this the next phase
of your education:

stop signaling in that way
that white poets often do
to the violence as if they were collecting
black bodies for themselves.
Their names were never yours in life,
and now they sure as fuck
don't belong to you in death.
So unless you plan on doing the work
—the real work—
to keep that long list of names
from growing:
Sandra Bland, Eric Garner, Michael Brown, Tamir Rice, Tanisha
don't you dare speak their names.
Don't you dare disturb their families' grief
with your unnecessary carelessness,
white in its largeness and self-importance.

You know this shit from your school days:
the distance between the signifier and signified
can be large,
but believe me when I tell you that—
in this instance—
for you—it's even larger.
So pay attention, you might learn something
if you just shut up for a moment and listen.
Trust me,
it's the very least you could do.

I

Letter 10

Dear I,

Initially, I wanted to respond
this way:
How dare you—
a highway that killed 3,000 people this year alone—
tell me
that I need to brush up on my semiotics.
Notice that the number doesn't include
all those assaulted by police & citizens alike,
all those trafficked, all those smuggling
the white powder, easily cut into lines
more defined than our borders.
Fuck you. How dare you assume my sins
as weighty as yours.

When my anger finally subsided,
I found myself white with guilt,
Anderson, Akai Gurley,   & wanted to grab you & shake you,
tell you:
You're right, oh god, you're right.
Absolve me
for I am that white woman
who called someone the wrong name,
who othered another when I had the chance,
who insisted on being first, before all others—
& these are the least of my sins.
Comfort me, oh god, for I am a sinner.

It was sincere—I was wrecked with it—
but it did nothing. Those tears were useless
& meant nothing. Guilt is useless
unless it reconciles
ourselves with ourselves
& with each other.

So now, I respond this way:
with my life, & a question:
how to reconcile?

M

Letter 11

M,

Do you remember
the panic that ran
through you when
the Minneapolis Bridge
collapsed?

You were hours away
in Iowa. You called,
everyone you loved
was okay. Believe me
when I tell you that you
will never know a more
profound failure
than I did that day.

I play a particular
role in the world:
I am the way—the means.
I ferry the living
& the dying
to their destinations—
a business God never
expressed interest in.
Even eternity has its
outsourcing.

Whatever your failures
may be—take comfort
that you are neither
the way nor the destination.
& unlike God, without you
& your fellow travelers—
I have no purpose.

Yours,
I

Letter 12

Dear I,

I read your note
as it down-poured,
nearly flooding here.
I'm sad for you.

I don't know
what it is to be
good anymore.
I thought you
could show me,
but you are only
the way.

At least
I have a few tiny hopes
& your hand.

M

Letter 13

Dear M,

It's been so long.

I picked up this postcard
from an antique shop
in Oklahoma,
thought of you.

I'm a tired, tired asshole,
M, I've stretched
too far. I'm all achy,
old, and falling apart.

I

FLASH FLOOD WARNING:
TURN AROUND
DON'T DROWN

Letter 14

Dear I,

The day started fine.
I did all the right
things: went to a party,
ate grilled burgers, drank
local beer, & played board
games with a family (a real one!
both parents & siblings present)
on an outdoor table in a real
backyard where the all-too-real
flies fed on crust, meat juice
& left over watermelon.
But, it wasn't just me. We
made extra efforts to engage
in the usual small talk
of strangers with nothing
in common but the generosity
of their host.

We pursued more right things,
all-American things: bought
fireworks, played pool
at the Black Sheep where we
drank more beer. & nothing
happened, not even fireworks
(as far as I was concerned).
I was in bed before midnight,
windows closed, applying
to renew my passport. See?
All the right things,
all the right things.

M

Letter 15

M,

Just south of Kansas City,
families pulled over on my shoulder,
stood stupidly outside to watch
the fireworks on Independence
Day while you were already sleeping.
Children were told not to pick up
anything from my collection of found-objects,
"that's dirty—don't touch that"
"don't pick that up—it's trash"
resonated in the mouths of so many parents.
This happens a lot, actually,
but that conversation usually involves
a flat tire or other vehicular inconveniences.
So much of what I am & do is
"dirty—" my work, my being, my collection
of broken, abandoned, & lost things.
Dirty. Dirty. Dirty.

But, don't feel so bad—
we're all rotten sometimes.

I

STALLED VEHICLE AHEAD

Letter 16

Dear I,

My roommate brought home
a bouquet of cotton for me.
Said she wasn't sure if I'd
ever seen it on the stem before
as a Northerner. She had pulled
over after the first Aggies football
game, & thought to climb
into a stranger's field for the sake
of sharing: the flowers, the white-
matted bolls, the brutish wire
of the stems so disproportionate
to the volume of harvest, of fruit,
of bounty. So deceptive—its gain
so light. Somehow, I channel all life
elsewhere, too.

This is the—my problem. This is why
I think of heaven as clouds
& not stems in the hearty earth.

M

Letter 17

Dear M,

January, Rain, & that Cold Front
got together for poker.
Those jokers love to spill
themselves over other people's lives.
What assholes.

They get together at the worst times.
Like the day I tried to get her back,
or the day you moved
& several when you didn't
have a jacket, remember?

But, it gets worse. February joins late
with a handle of whiskey & a wad
of cash from panhandling
out by where 290 & I meet to trash talk.
Some hipster with a Krishna tattoo
around her shoulder & bug-eyed glasses,
all slouched over the wheel of her jeep
hands him a few $50s—
mumbling something about karma.
Sounded high as fuck.
February said, "God bless you—
I mean—Namaste"
as she drove off.
Lucky fuck.

Keep your jumper cables handy,

I

Letter 18

Dear I,

You sound rough. Hold these comforts:
that some of those boys & girls
from our Midwest are hunting deer,
trying to stay warm & still.
Trying to hold a piss in early morning,
while I sleep in Texas.

Another comfort: as I write you,
living rooms are filling with cold beer & chili
because of the Superbowl. & you & I
are somewhere—making valentines,
sleeping in, or cleaning—not giving a fuck
about what's on a screen in our respective haunts.

The Super Bowl is like Poetry is like Death—
the thing is not about itself. It's multiplicity.
Sometimes, pride, or language, but not Death—
the things that leads Death—the crack
of hardened branches, the mad dash
through white, right beneath the quiet Death.

Knowing you (& all the parts I don't—
which you so often love to remind me of
but I will never cease looking for),
I wait for your dismemberment.

M

Letter 19

Dear M,

Is everything okay?
Haven't heard from you
in a while.

I wrote, but maybe
you never received my last letter?

I don't wanna hash it
all out all over again.
Death is too ridiculous
a topic for conversation—
poetry too—too dark
for my taste. You missed
a hellova game, though.

Tell me everything—
but mostly about
your time in Duluth,
my colder half.
There's something
I want to hear about.

I

PASS
WITH
CARE

Letter 20

Dear I,

I'm sorry it's been so long,
even after your sweet request.
Early spring has me blue.

Do you remember last July?

Peter, Hannah & I drove to Duluth
to snag you by the tail—did you feel it?
Can you feel the reverberations now—
you long-necked, urban beast?
I feel your slither—I'll be your handler,
the kindest because I see your nature
& love it.

I kid, of course. We didn't find a tail,
but your mouth. & feathers
—not yours, but the birds' who shit
on the cement barriers lining
the slow ease into Lake Superior
where we went looking for a lighthouse
we could never get to; it was inaccessible
from where we hiked. So we settled
for a new destination: an old, graffitied post.
A skinny, long cement plank into water
led us straight to the post, the birds acting
as a funeral procession for our bodies—
flying before us & landing
on the barrier after we passed them.
I want life like that—everything buffered
by a clamor, feathers, fury.
I'd manage even the harshest of your blows
under the condition that—before & after—
I can come up for air.

M

Letter 21

Dear M,

No one thinks about
what is required
to be clean.
It requires a mouth saying,
"Don't worry, I got this."
"Go bathe."
"Go rest"
or "Let me get that for you,"
with a hand.
It requires someone
to break through my body,
picking it clean
of the shit entangled
in my hair & limbs,
like crows on a carcass.

The work is never over,
not even the work
I've tasked you:
be ready —always—
in words and actions.
Rest in spirts.

But there's no rest for me.
& there is no one
who can stop what's coming
or going.

I

REST AREA ¼ MILE

Micah Ruelle is a queer Midwestern poet. She holds a BA in English from the University of Central Missouri, an MFA from Texas State University, and a CPTS from Oxford University's Wycliffe Hall, where she studied theology. She has been published in journals such as the *Chicago Quarterly Review, Cutthroat, Profane, About Place,* and others. She currently resides in the Kansas City area with her cat, Gabe.